Best Origami Christmas Ornaments to Make with Your Kids

6 Adorable and Easy Patterns

Table of Content

Introduction

Try these origami Christmas ornaments. They cost very little to make and you're guaranteed that the kids will enjoy making their own Christmas tree decorations and learn a thing or two along the way. From ornaments, to santa, to lucky stars, wreath, card and baubles, there is something for everyone.

The season of snow flurry has ceased, and the heaviest snow has blanketed the backyard. There is a possibility that a fierce snowstorm will hit the town soon. You and your little ones are glued to the window hoping for a ray of sunlight to melt the ice. They have already made dozens of snowmen, and it is too risky to drive to ice-skating ring. It looks like you guys will have to stay at home for a while.

Origami Santa

This easy origami Father Christmas is a great origami project for kids over the winter holidays.

You only need one sheet of square paper for this origami Santa. Preferably it will have a red and a white side. If you don't have any of this kind of origami paper, simply just use plain white printer paper and color in the red sections after it's folded.

Children may need some help with this origami model at first, but kids aged 8+ should be able to fold it once and get the hang of it.

MATERIALS

- 1 piece 7.8- x 7.8-inch paper (20 x 20 centimeters)
- Glue (optional)
- Wool
- Heavy book (optional)
- Black pen
- Pink pen

- White pen

INSTRUCTIONS

Step 1: Create Creases

Start with your paper with the colored (red) side facing upward. Fold the paper in half, from bottom to top and from left to right. You will now have a neat cross.

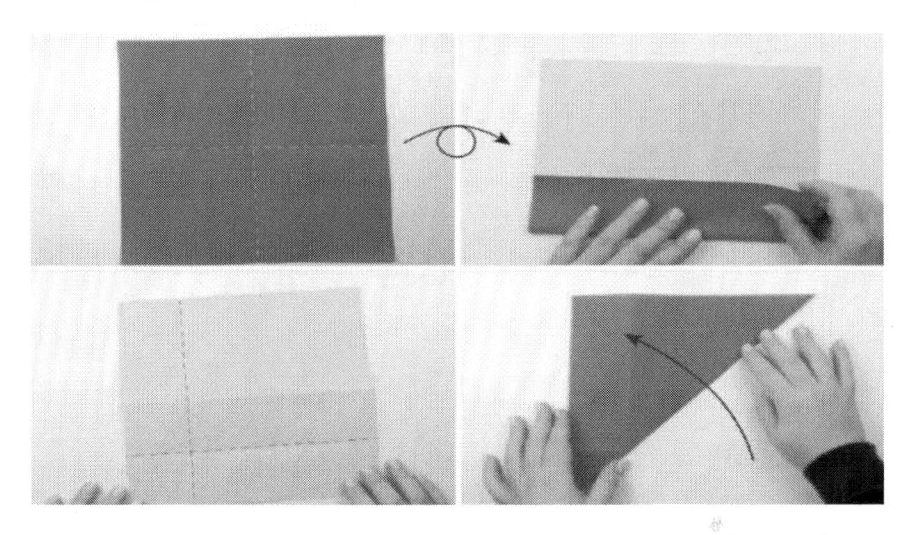

Flip the paper over to the other side (white side). Fold the bottom edge up to meet the horizontal crease and unfold. Fold the left edge to meet the vertical central crease and unfold. Fold the bottom right corner up to the top left corner, then unfold.

Step 2: Rotate and Fold

Rotate the paper so that the diagonal line is vertically centered and flip the paper over to the other side. Check to make sure that your paper is the same as indicated. Fold the bottom section up as shown and unfold. Fold the bottom corner up to the previous crease and unfold.

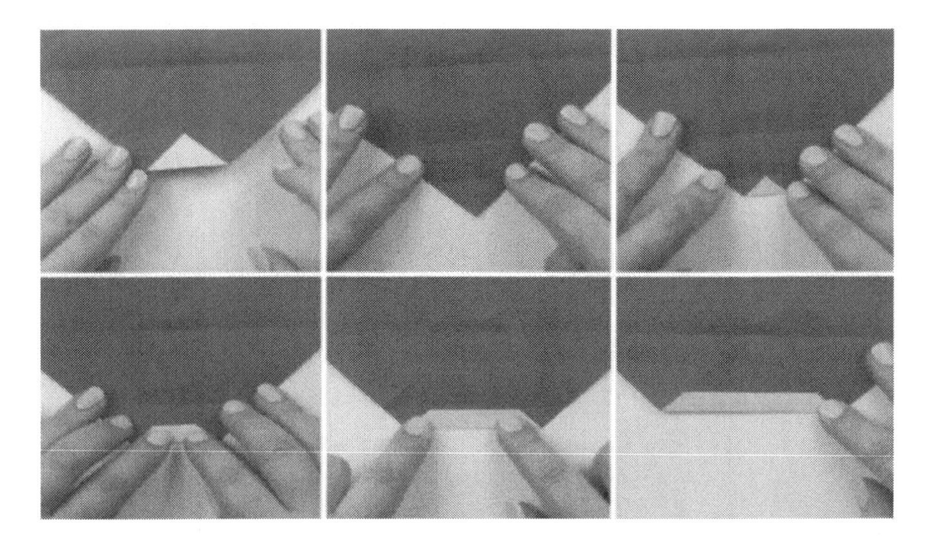

Step 3: Continue to Fold.

Fold the bottom corner up to the crease you just made. Unfold. Fold the bottom corner up again to the crease you just made. Flip the bottom section up. Flip it up again, and fold it up once more.

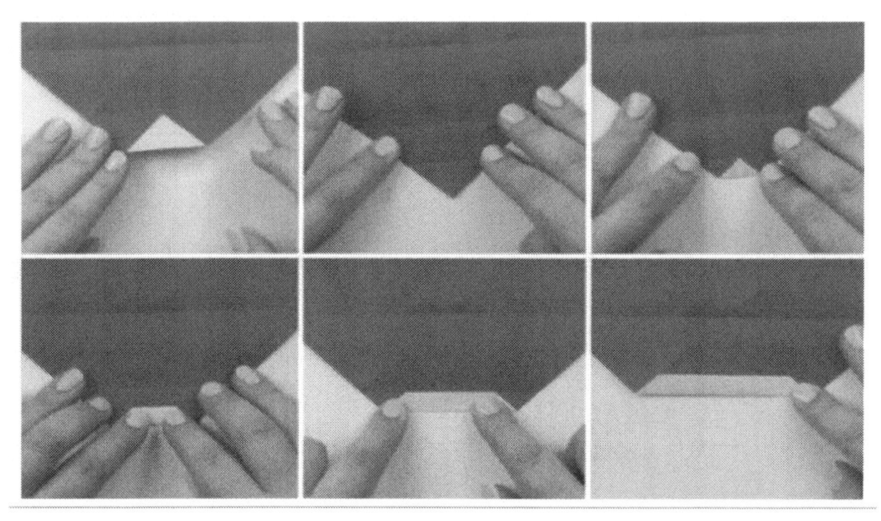

Step 4: Flip the Paper Over

Flip the paper over to the other side, and rotate the paper so that the folded corner is now at the top. Bring the top left and right sections in towards the middle. Collapse the top section down and fold well. Fold the bottom corner up to the top corner.

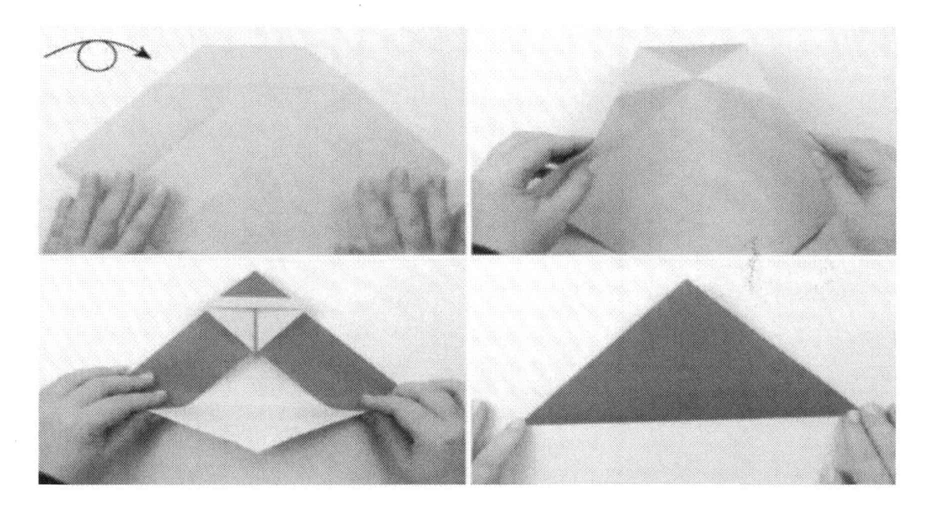

Step 5: Make Santa's Hat and Beard

Fold the top corner down, leaving a small gap between Santa's hat and his beard. Fold another small section down, creating Santa's mustache. Flip the paper over to the other side. Fold the bottom right corner up to the top corner.

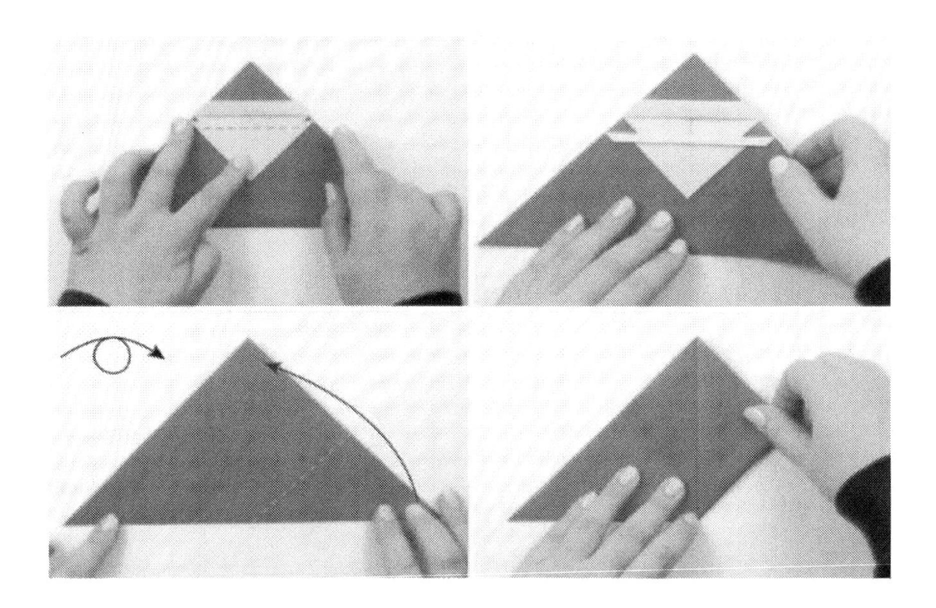

Step 6: Finish Folding Your Santa

Fold the bottom left section up to the top corner. Fold the right edge to the center, folding all of the layers. Fold the left section the same way. Fold the bottom corner up a little bit, completing your origami Santa!

You can use some glue to stick the back down, or you can leave it inside a heavy book overnight and it will be flat in the morning.

Step 7: Decorate the Santa

Now it's time to decorate it. Use a black pen for his eyes, a pink pen for the nose, a white pen for the buttons, and a small ball of wool for the top of Santa's hat.

Origami Christmas Tree Card

Learn how to make a wonderful origami Christmas tree card! A handmade Christmas card is the perfect finishing touch to your gifts this Christmas!

This super simple origami Christmas tree is made using 4 sheets of small square paper.

You will need a few dabs of glue to complete the finished Christmas tree card!

The sizes used for the card in the photo are 7.5 x 7.5 cm thin card. You can use any kind of paper you have around the house.

MATERIALS

- 4 7.5x7.5-centimeter cardstock
- Glue

INSTRUCTIONS

Step 1: Get Started. Starting white side up (if you have one). Fold the paper in half diagonally both ways. Flip the paper over to the other (colored) side and rotate. Fold the paper in half and unfold.

Step 2: Make the Pieces of the Tree. Flip the paper back over to the other side. Push the right and left sides into the middle, collapsing the top section down. You now have a water bomb base. Make two more of these.

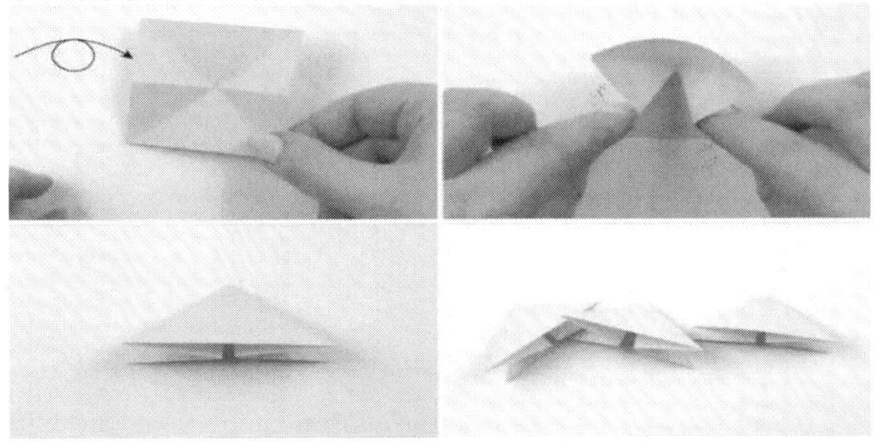

Step 3: Make the Tree Trunk. Now it's time to make the trunk of the origami Christmas tree. Start white side up (if you have one). Fold the paper in half both ways and unfold. Flip the paper to the other side. Fold the bottom right corner up to the top left corner. Unfold.

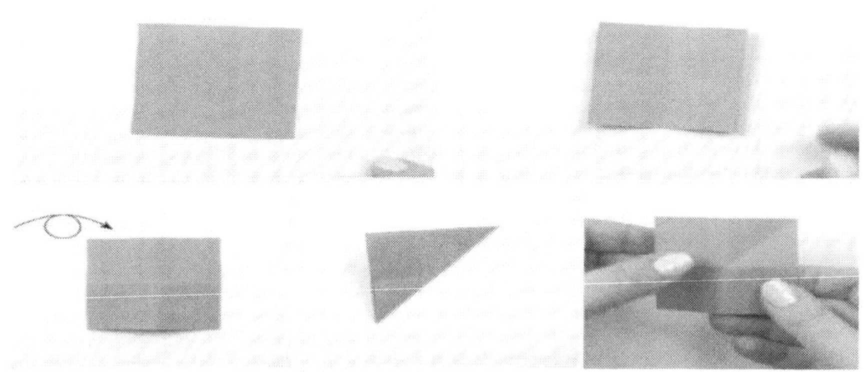

Step 4: Continue Folding the Trunk. Rotate the paper and flip it over to the other side. Push in the right and left corners to the middle. This is an origami square base.

Fold the right and left corners to the middle. Fold the bottom corner up to the middle and unfold. Repeat on the back.

Step 5: Glue the Tree Together. Now it's time to stick the tree together with a bit of glue. Glue the top of one of the tree sections.

Get another tree section and slot it on top, gluing it at the same time. You can adjust the height of the tree by pushing it on further. Do the same with the tree trunk.

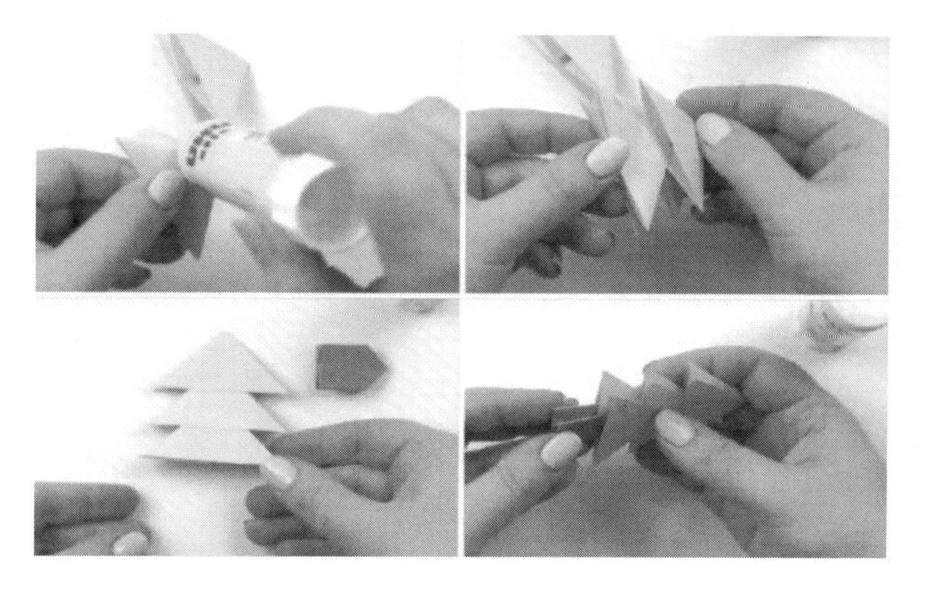

Step 6: Attach the Tree to a Card. Now you can stick the tree onto a piece of card that is folded in half. Leave the tree as it is or make it more three dimensional by folding the right and left sections in the opposite directions.

You can also decorate the tree by drawing baubles and tinsel with pens or sticking other decorations on top!

Origami Lucky Stars

Learn how to make lovely little origami lucky stars, sometimes called wishing stars. Use them as party decorations, add color to a room, add them to gift wrap, or use them to add a little luck to your life. Make one or dozens of cute little stars with this step-by-step tutorial.

These origami lucky stars are made with strips of paper cut about 10-inches to 11-inches long. Each strip can be as wide as 1/4 inch, 1/2 inch, or 3/4 inch. Thinner strips make smaller stars while fatter strips make larger stars.

Spend as much time as is needed to make the knot and wrap the pentagon of your star as neat and tight as possible. Making it neat ensures your little origami lucky stars will turn out puffy, but sturdy, as well if you want to hold them while making a wish.

MATERIALS

- Printer paper, A4 paper, letter paper, patterned paper, or origami paper

- Paper cutter or scissors
- Ruler

INSTRUCTIONS

Step 1: Start Folding the Strip of Paper

- ➢ Start with your strip of paper color side up if you're using colored paper or origami paper.
- ➢ Bring the right end of the paper over and down.
- ➢ Bring the bottom end up and over the left end.
- ➢ Now that you have a loop, feed the top end behind and through the hole.
- ➢ Continue to pull the end through the loop, also gently pull the bottom end to tighten the knot.

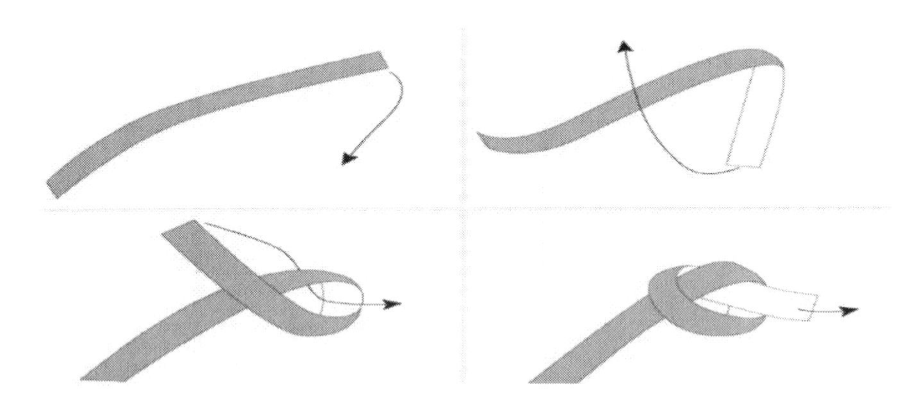

Step 2: Make the Knot of the Star

- ➢ Keep wiggling and pulling the knot tighter, flattening it at the same time.
- ➢ The end of the paper strip on the left should be much longer than the end on the right. Fold the excess end behind. You do not need to cut it off but you can do if it's too long.

- Fold the end on the left behind, keeping the bottom edge aligned with the bottom edge of the shape in the center.
- Continue wrapping the pentagon. Fold the strip on top, over to the top left.

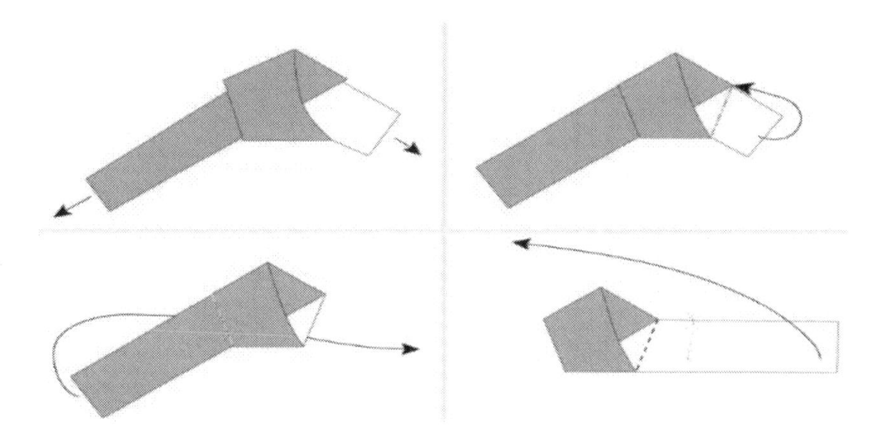

Step 3: Keep Wrapping the Pentagon

- Again wrapping the pentagon, fold the strip down behind to the bottom.
- Fold the strip up and over to the right.
- Fold the strip over behind to the left and continue until you only have a small section left.
- If your strip is just a bit too long, cut it or tear it off.

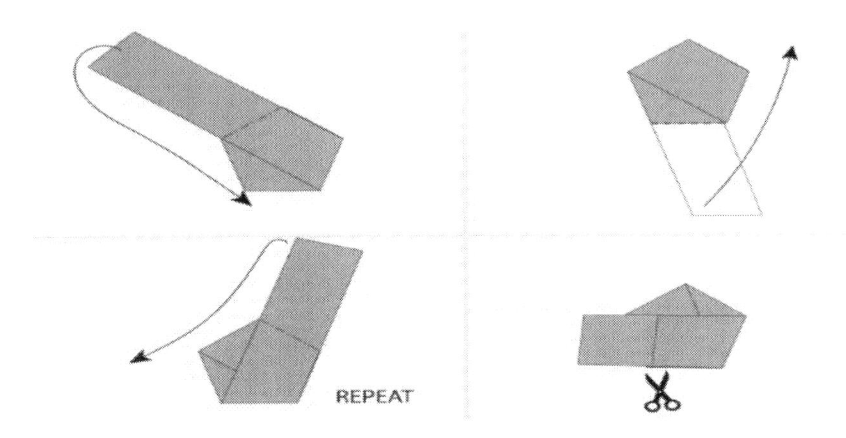

Step 4: Finish Tucks and Inflate the Star

- Insert the end of the strip inside the pocket.
- Now inflate the star. Use your index finger and thumb to pinch in one of the points of the star.
- Rotate the star and gently do the same on all of the points.
- You can get different results by pinching more or less at this stage.

Your first attempt at making an origami star may not come out as well as expected, but keep practicing to create the points.

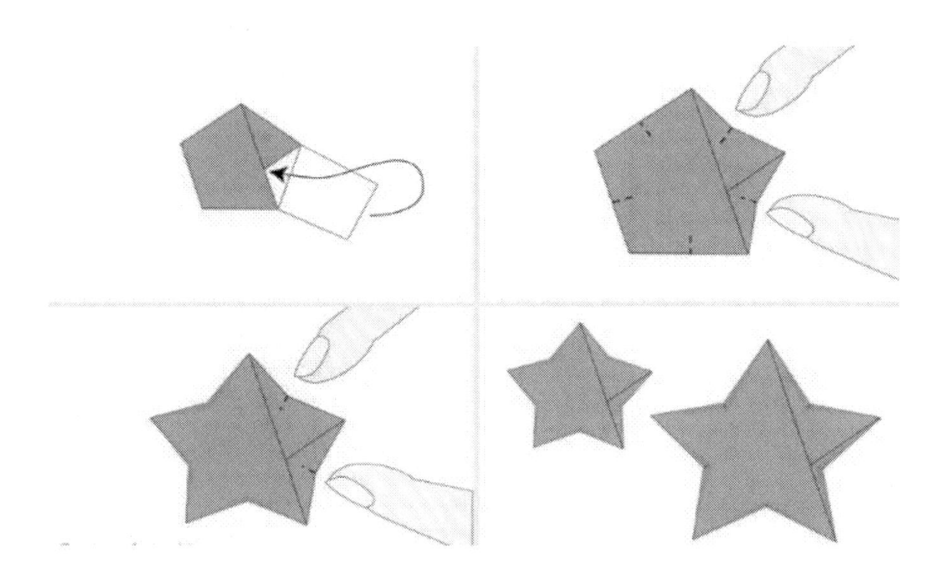

Origami Christmas Baubles

These handmade paper Christmas decorations are not only cost-effective, but they look absolutely stunning. With a couple of packs of origami paper, scissors, glue, a dash of patience and some ribbon, you'll have your very own bespoke paper Christmas baubles!

MATERIALS

- Origami papers (or very thin paper)
- Scissors
- PVA glue and a small brush
- Thin ribbon

Large decorations – use 2 x 21cm paper squares
Small decorations – use 2 x 17cm paper squares

INTRODUCTIONS

Step 1: Take one square of paper. Fold diagonally in half, then open it out.

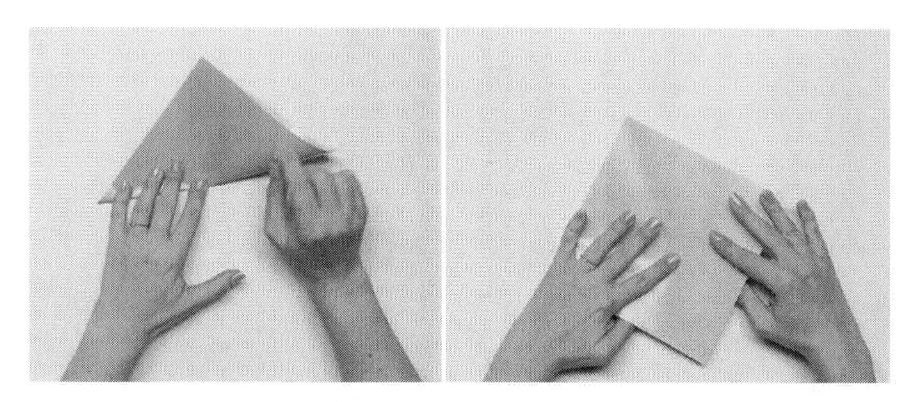

Step 2: Fold the square diagonally in half the other way, this time keeping it folded.

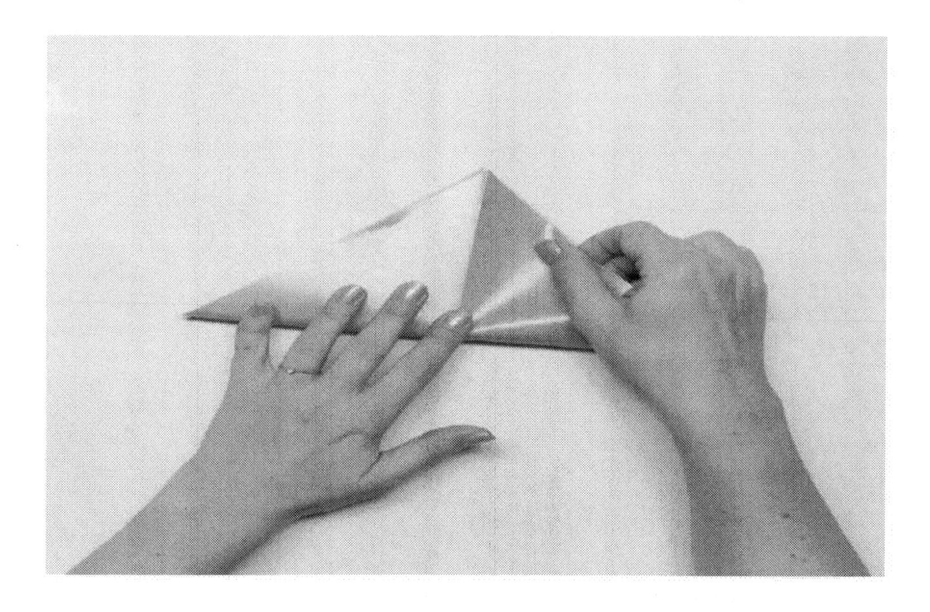

Step 3: With the base of the triangle towards you, take the right point down to the bottom point and fold.

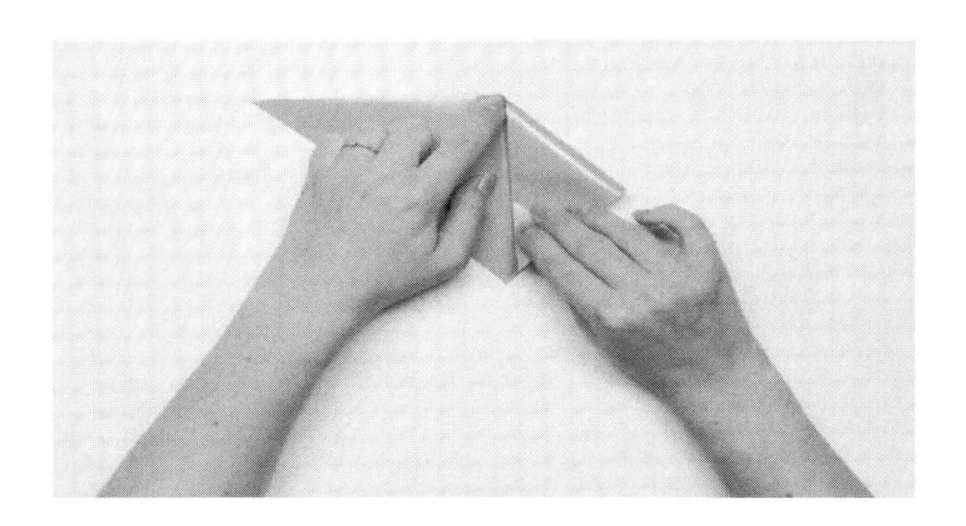

Step 4: Repeat this, by taking the left point down to the bottom point, and fold.

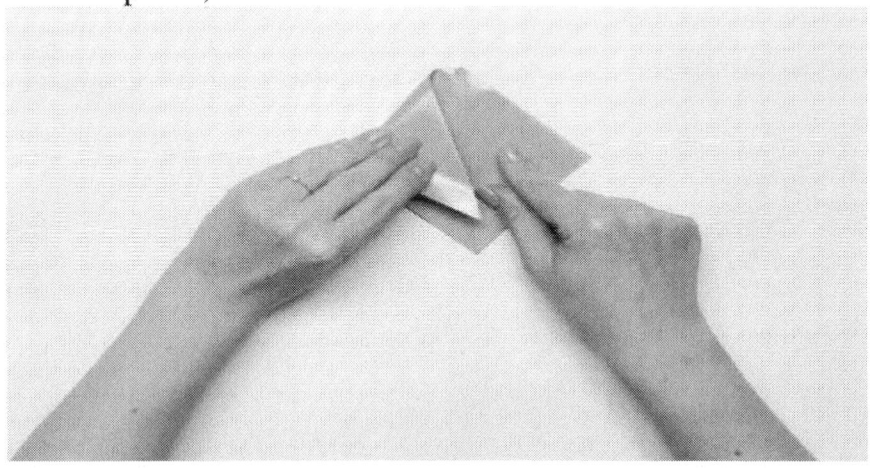

Step 5: Turn the diamond shape around 180°. Open out the left side of the diamond. Fold the inner piece over to the right, then press along the crease

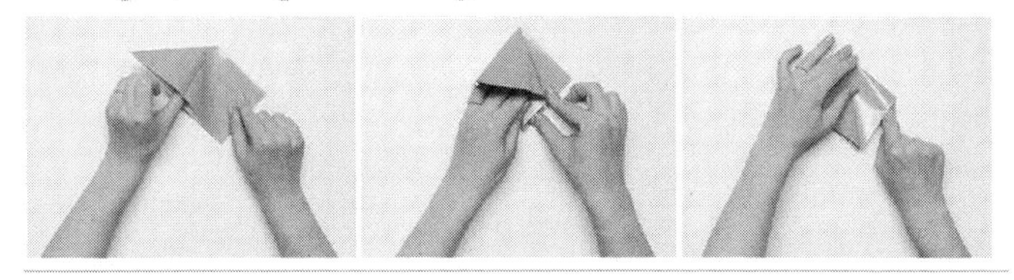

Step 6: Do the same on the other side. With the open side of the diamond facing away from you, fold in the two sides to the central crease to create a kite shape.

Step 7: Flip over and do the same on the other side. Cut off the excess triangles from the top.

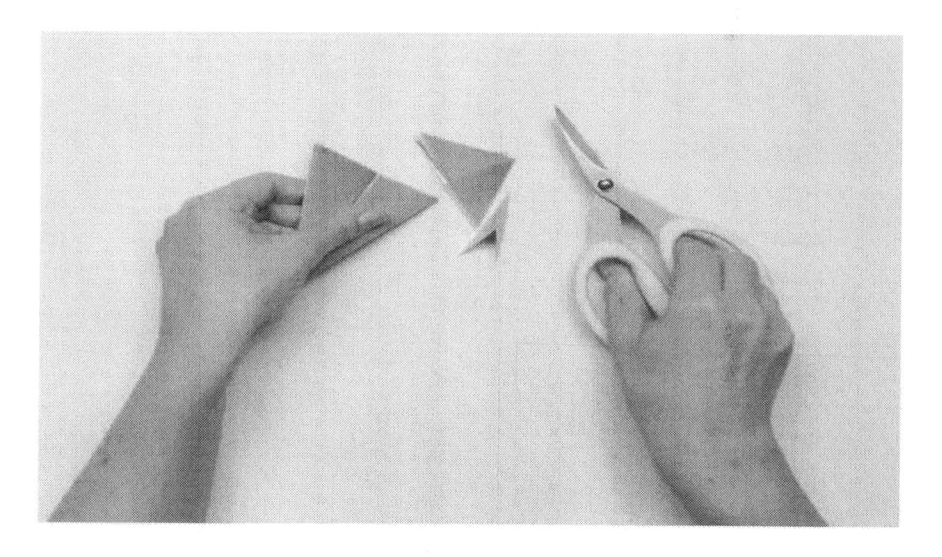

Step 8: With the base of the triangle facing towards you, use the same technique as in Step Six. Open out a section, fold the inner piece to the right and press along the crease.

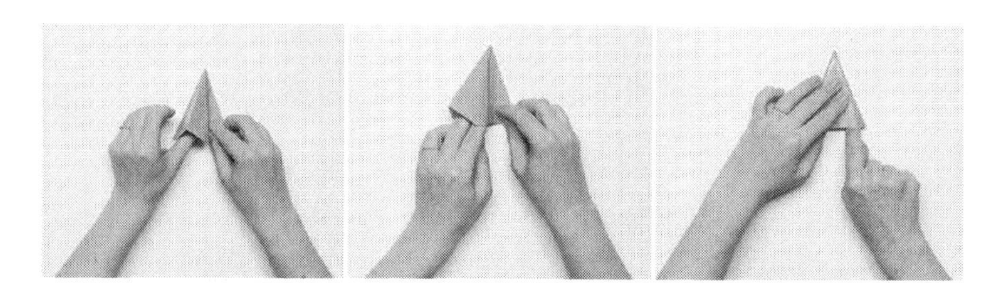

Step 9: Repeat this technique to all of the sections. With the base of the triangle towards you, take the right point and fold it up to along the central crease.

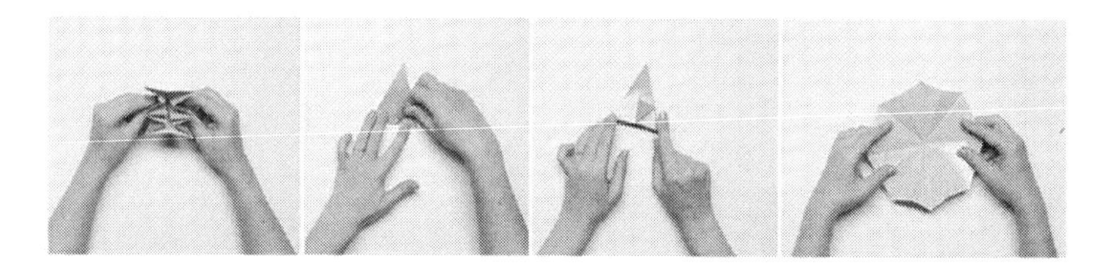

Step 10: Repeat this technique to all of the points.
Open out the shape. Fold the small triangles you've just created inwards, and crease. Do this all the way around and place to one side.

Step 11: Repeat this whole process to create a second identical shape.

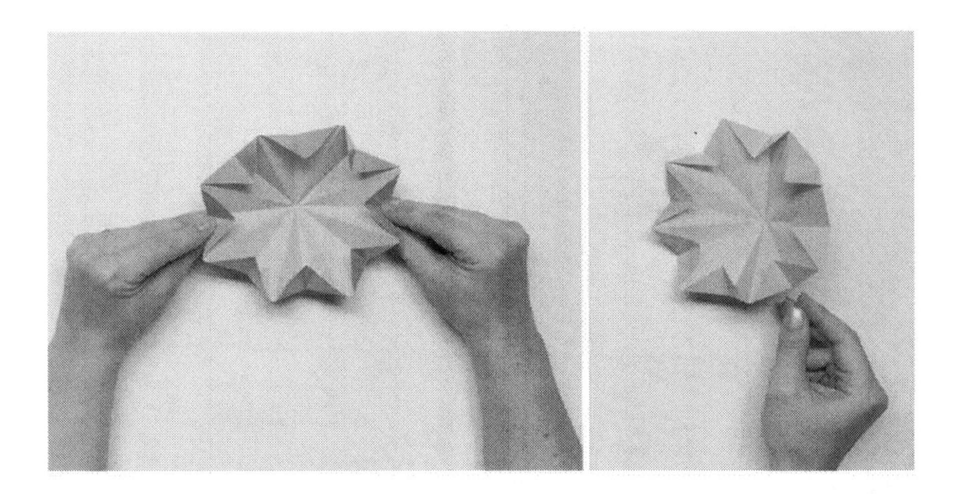

Step 12: Cut a 25cm length of thin ribbon or twine and thread it onto a large needle. Cut a small slit in the centre of one of the shapes and thread the ribbon through the hole, then back down again.

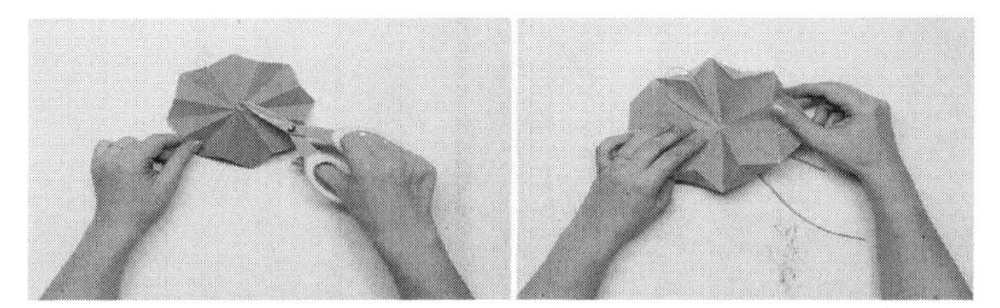

Step 13: Take off the needle. Tie a large knot into the ribbon (you don't want it coming up through the hole you just made) Apply a little glue to the knot to secure it.

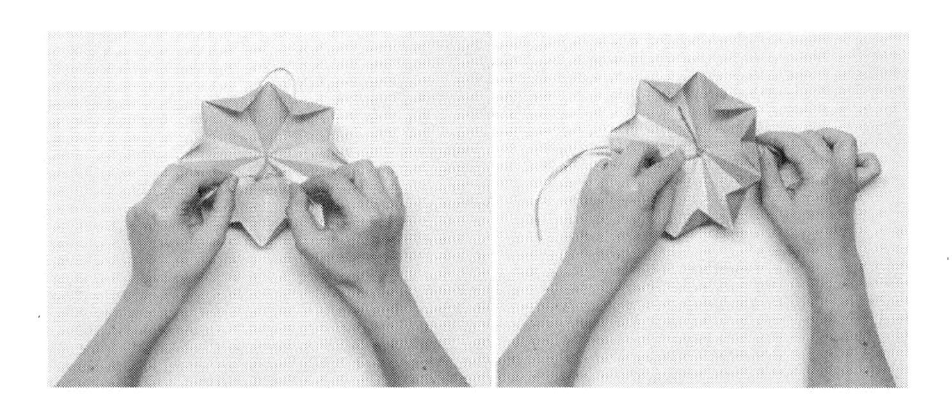

Step 14: Apply some glue to 2 of the points of one paper shapes. Take the other paper shape, line up the points and hold in place until secure.

Step 15: Continue gluing around the edges, 2 or 3 points at a time, until you have created one whole shape. Leave to dry.

TIP: It's a good idea to work on gluing a few decorations at once, say 4 or 5, as by the time you have glued a couple of sections of them all, the first one will be strong enough to work on again

Step 16: Finishing

Origami Christmas Wreath

Normally people make Christmas wreaths from evergreens, because plants that survive winter symbolise the strength of life.

I'll show you a slightly unconventional (but still beautiful) way to make Christmas wreaths... from paper.

MATERIALS

- Colorful paper or card
- A pencil
- A ruler
- Scissors

INSTRUCTIONS

Step 1: Cut out 8 rectangles from coloured card or paper. Each rectangle should be twice as long as it is wide. If you're using paper, then you can start with squares instead, and fold them in half to make rectangles.

Step 2: Pick one of the rectangles, and fold it in half lengthwise, so that the fold is toward you and the cut edges are away from you.

Step 3 : Fold the top corners down to meet the bottom edge.

Step 4: Fold in half like this.

Step 5: Fold all the other pieces the same way.

Step 6: Take a close look at one of the pieces. There are two "slots", where another piece can slide into it. I've widened them here to make them obvious.

Step 7: Fit two pieces together like this. The two prongs on the red piece fit into the two slots on the green piece.

Step 8: Continue slotting all the pieces together. Tadaa! You have a wreath! Add a ribbon and hang it on your tree.

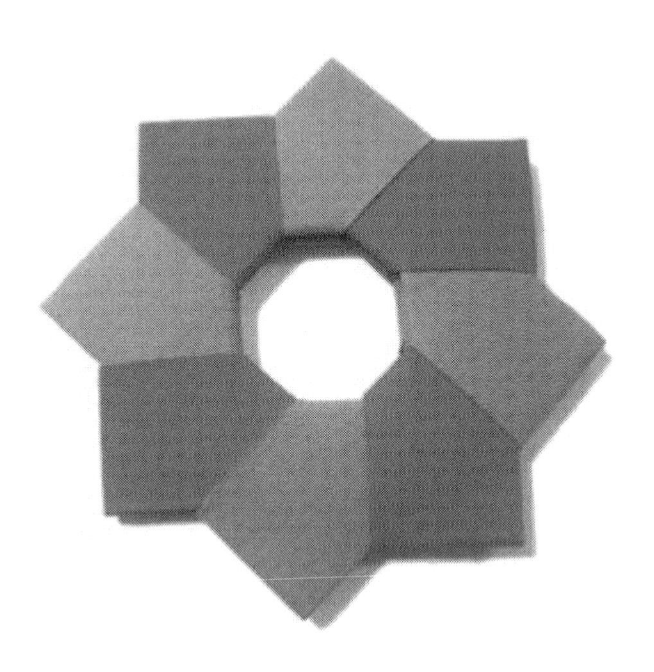

Origami German Bell

Isn't this a pretty little ornament? Considering how quickly the days until Christmas are flying by, I bet you'll be happy to hear the directions to make one are surprisingly simple.

MATERIALS

- Index cards or lightweight card stock or heavyweight vellum
- Paper cutter
- Ruler
- Bone folder - for sharp creases
- Sissors
- Double-stick tape

- Quick-drying glue - suitable for paper
- Acrylic paint - gold or silver
- Stencil brush
- Beads - gold, silver, white
- Ornament cord - metallic gold or silver

INSTRUCTIONS

Step 1: Cut a 5 x 5-inch square. Fold the square in half.

Step 2: Open the square, turn the paper ninety degrees and fold in half again.

Step 3: Open the square and fold two corners point to point.

Step 4: Open the square and fold the remaining two corners point to point.

Step 5: Open the square and make an airplane fold at each corner. Do this by bringing the paper on each side of the fold line to the midline and creasing.

Each corner with its airplane fold will look like this:

Make sure to open each airplane fold after you have creased the two sides before going on to airplane fold the next corner.

Step 6: After all four corners have been folded, open the square and press the space between each airplane fold... the square will begin to look like this:

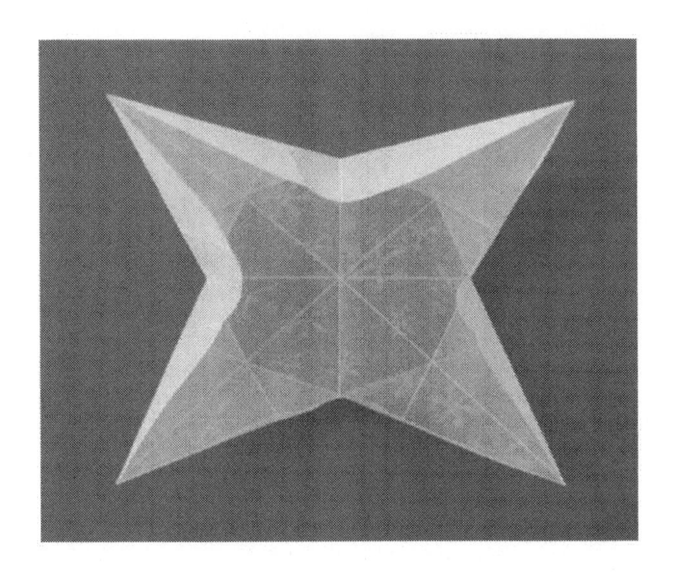

Step 7: Cup the paper in the palm of one hand and gently press in on the center with the fingers of your other hand... this will convince the bell to take shape.

If you have successfully completed all of the folds, the four points will spring up and you'll be holding a bell!

Step 8: Make a hanging loop of ornament cord (about 10 inches) and knot the end after stringing on a bead or beads. Make another knot or two at the top of the beads so they won't slide off the loop.

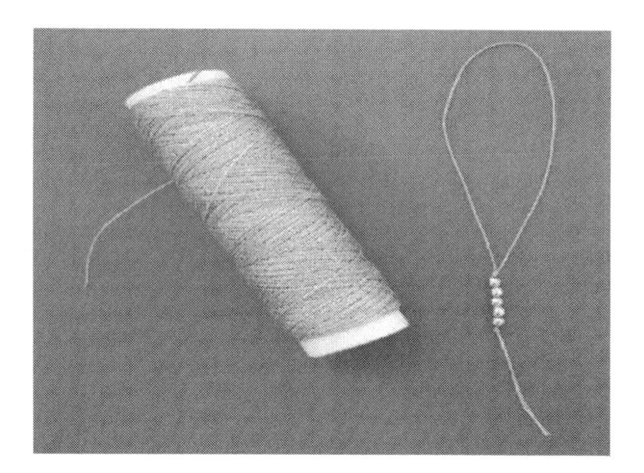

Step 9: Apply narrow strips of double-stick tape to the inside of the bell along each of the airplane folds. Adhere the tail of the hanging loop to one of the pieces of tape.

Gently press the outside of the bell... the tape pieces will stick to one another, holding the bell closed.

Step 10: Add a dab of quick-drying glue just inside the tip to make sure the bell won't pop open.

Tip: I find it's best to use tape along the airplane folds as extra security when working with vellum, but if you are using an index card or card stock, a bit of glue where the four corner points come together will most likely be all the adhesion that is needed.

Made in the USA
Middletown, DE
25 November 2022